BUGGED OUT!
The World's Most Dangerous Bugs

FILTHY FLIES

by Alex Giannini

Consultant: Paula L. Marcet, PhD
Research Biologist
Atlanta, Georgia

BEARPORT
PUBLISHING

New York, New York

Credits

Cover, © egiss/iStock; TOC, © irin-k/Shutterstock; 4L, © Ana Gram/Shutterstock; 4R, © Riana Van Staden/ Dreamstime; 5L, © Science Source; 5R, © Kim Taylor/NPL/Minden Pictures; 6, © Indiapicture/Alamy; 7T, © John A.L. Cook/Animals Animals/AGE Fotostock; 7B, © Jacobeukman/iStock; 8TL, © Stockfotocz/ Dreamstime; 8TR, © StevenEllingson/iStock; 8B, © annop youngrot/Shutterstock; 9, © Lawrence Reeves; 10L, © Ivalin/Shutterstock; 10R, © Guilliam Lopez/Camera Press/Redux Pictures; 11, © Amazon-Images/ Alamy; 12, © royaltystockphoto.com/Shutterstock; 13T, © MYN/Gil Wizen/Minden Pictures; 13B, © Piotr Naskrecki/Minden Pictures; 14L, © Sopotnicki/Shutterstock; 14R, © Sightsavers; 15T, © blickwinkel/Alamy; 15B, © Mike Goldwater/Alamy; 16T, © Piotr Naskrecki/Minden Pictures/AGE Fotostock; 16B, © zabelin/ iStock; 17, © ANT Photo Library/Science Source; 18L, © Joubert/Phanie/AGE Fotostock; 18R, © PT1/Wenn/ Newscom; 19, © khlungcenter/Shutterstock; 20, © Skinny_Dog/iStock; 21T, © Ranta Images/Shutterstock; 21B, © Panupong Ponchai/Dreamstime; 22 (T to B), © Billion Photos/Shutterstock, © Oxford Media Library/ Shutterstock, and © jxfzsy/iStock.

Publisher: Kenn Goin
Senior Editor: Joyce Tavolacci
Creative Director: Spencer Brinker
Photo Researcher: Thomas Persano

Library of Congress Cataloging-in-Publication Data

Names: Giannini, Alex, author.
Title: Filthy flies / by Alex Giannini.
Description: New York, New York : Bearport Publishing, [2019] | Series:
    Bugged out! the world's most dangerous bugs |
    Includes bibliographical references and index. | Description based on
    print version record and CIP data provided by publisher; resource not
    viewed.
Identifiers: LCCN 2018047336 (print) | LCCN 2018049050 (ebook) | ISBN
    9781642802368 (ebook) | ISBN 9781642801675 (library)
Subjects: LCSH: Flies as carriers of disease—Juvenile literature. |
    Tsetse-flies—Juvenile literature.
Classification: LCC RA641.T7 (ebook) | LCC RA641.T7 G54 2019 (print) | DDC
    595.77/4—dc23
LC record available at https://lccn.loc.gov/2018047336

For more information, write to Bearport Publishing Company, Inc., 45 West 21st Street, Suite 3B, New York, New York 10010. Printed in the United States of America.

10 9 8 7 6 5 4 3 2 1

Contents

A Strange Sickness

Erich Burger couldn't wait to go on an African **safari**. In 2016, he and his family traveled from their home in Maryland to Botswana and Zambia. However, Erich's dream vacation turned into a nightmare the day after he got home. Erich came down with a fever, rash, and severe body aches. Over the next couple weeks, he became so tired and weak he could barely stand up.

Erich Burger saw lions and many other animals on safari in Africa.

Erich went to the hospital, where doctors ordered tests to check for different diseases. When lab worker Gail Wilson looked at his blood under a **microscope**, she saw tiny worm-like **parasites**. "I knew it was serious and that the patient could die," Gail said. Erich had sleeping sickness—a rare and potentially **fatal** disease carried by tsetse (TSET-see) flies!

A pair of tsetse flies

The deadly parasites in Erich's blood can be seen in the photograph above, in dark pink. The bacteria-spreading parasites attack the central nervous system and can cause sleepiness, confusion, and death.

Sleeping sickness is also called African trypanosomiasis (trih-pan-uh-soh-MAHY-uh-sis).

Dead Asleep

At the hospital, doctors rushed to help Erich. However, the treatment for sleeping sickness can be **toxic**. In fact, five to ten percent of patients die from it. Erich had no choice but to try the risky treatment—his life depended on it. Luckily for Erich, the drugs started working, and he slowly began to recover.

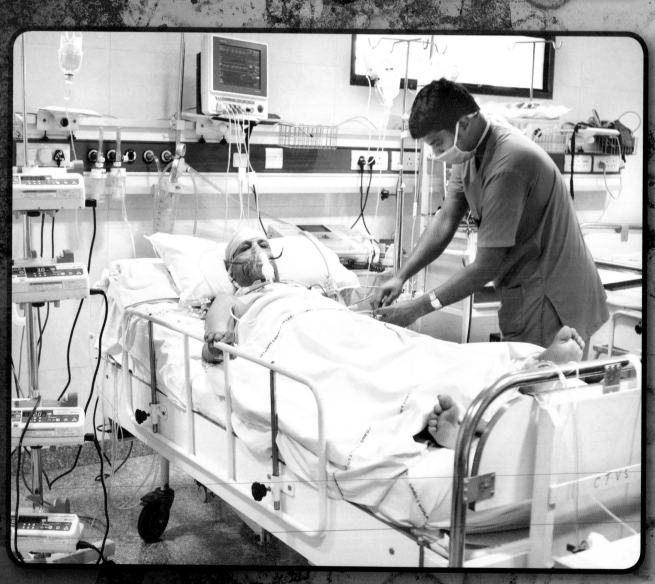

Erich stayed in a hospital much like this one for seven days.

How did Erich get sleeping sickness? Doctors think he was bitten by a tsetse fly while viewing wildlife in Africa. Erich recalls seeing flies buzzing around him but doesn't remember the actual bite. When asked if he'd go back to Africa, Erich said: "I'm not going to stop traveling because a fly bit me."

Tsetse flies live in 36 different African countries. They have long mouthparts that can easily pierce through skin.

Tsetse flies feed on the blood of humans and other animals. They pick up the microscopic parasites that cause sleeping sickness by sucking an infected animal's blood.

This water buffalo is covered with tsetse flies. The insects got their name because their wings are said to make a *tse-tse* sound as they fly.

Attack of the Flies!

Flies are everywhere. In fact, there are more than 120,000 different kinds buzzing around. They range in size from tiny mosquitoes to large horseflies. Of these, there are two main groups. Biting flies, like the tsetse fly, feed on blood. Filth flies, such as the common housefly, feed on rotting foods, garbage, and even **manure**.

Horsefly

Fruit fly

Common housefly

One especially nasty **species** of biting fly is the botfly. This large, hairy insect lives in Central and South America. What really sets it apart is how it produces its young. First, a female lays her eggs on the body of a mosquito. When the mosquito bites a human or other **mammal**, the botfly eggs hatch. Then a **larva** crawls into the **wound** left by the mosquito. Finally, the baby botfly begins to feed on its victim's flesh!

Botfly larvae can stay under their host's skin for up to six weeks.

A mosquito carrying botfly eggs

Botfly eggs

Under the Skin

In 1973, a young scientist named Jerry Coyne had a very up-close **encounter** with a botfly. When Jerry was still a student, he traveled to Costa Rica in Central America. On one of the final days of his trip, Jerry and his classmates were walking through a forest. Suddenly, Jerry heard the buzzing sound of a mosquito. As he tried to swat the pest away, it bit the top of his head.

Jerry Coyne

A waterfall in Costa Rica

Jerry soon realized this was no ordinary mosquito bite. After a couple of days, it swelled to the size of a pea. Jerry asked a classmate to take a look. When she did, she saw the tiny breathing tube poking out of the bite. "There is something moving in there!" she shouted. What was on the other end of the tube? Jerry knew it could only be one horrifying thing—a botfly **maggot**!

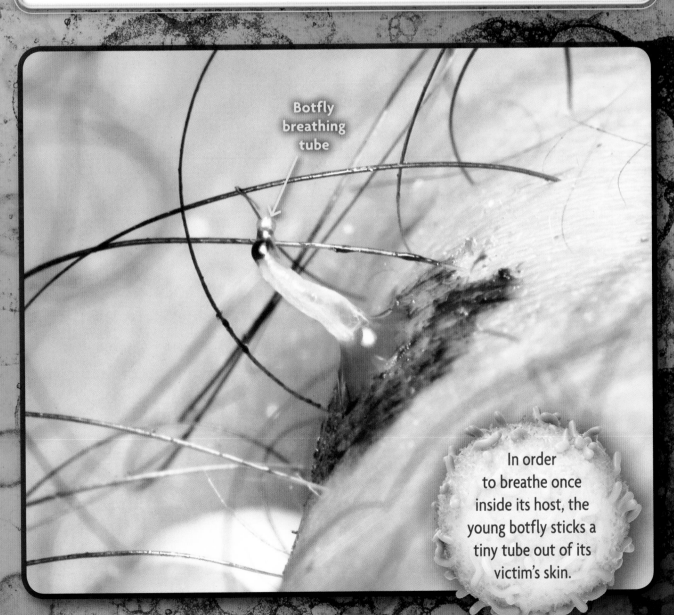

Botfly breathing tube

In order to breathe once inside its host, the young botfly sticks a tiny tube out of its victim's skin.

A Vile Visitor

Jerry knew that removing the maggot would be difficult and dangerous. Botfly larvae have a pair of hooks on their backside that dig into the skin. "If you try to pull the thing out, it just digs in and you'll break it in two," said Jerry. This could lead to a serious **infection**.

A computer illustration of a botfly maggot

Jerry decided to leave the maggot alone. "The botfly wasn't that painful, and I knew it was going to come out on its own," Jerry said. Weeks later, the bug bite on his head grew to the size of a small egg. Then one night the botfly crawled out of the bite! Jerry found a fat, white worm with tiny black teeth on his pillow. The bite eventually healed, but Jerry will never forget the alarming experience.

Jerry saved the maggot, hoping to raise it into an adult botfly, but it died.

A botfly larva and an adult botfly

A botfly exiting its host's skin

Blinded by a Blackfly

Blackflies are another kind of dangerous biting fly. John and Jean Wilson learned about them first-hand during a trip to Ghana in West Africa in 1950. At night, they noticed huge clouds of blackflies buzzing near a river. They also met hundreds of people blinded by those same flies. The Wilsons named the **devastating** illness river blindness—and devoted their lives to **eradicating** it.

John Wilson was blinded during an accident when he was 12 years old. This experience inspired him to help other blind people.

A river in Ghana, West Africa

Blackflies live and breed along rivers in tropical areas. Many carry parasitic worms called *Onchocerca volvulus*. Blackflies can transfer the worms to humans through a bite. A female worm might lay thousands of eggs inside a person. After the eggs hatch, the baby worms travel to the victim's skin or eyes. As the worms die, they cause terrible itching and **sores**. Worst of all, they can severely damage the eyes, leading to blindness.

A blackfly

In 1950, John and Jean Wilson started an organization called Sightsavers to help people affected by river blindness.

A person suffering from river blindness

The Baghdad Boil

Like blackflies, sand flies also carry a frightening disease. In 2010, Mason Alsaleh was an **interpreter** for the U.S. Army working in Iraq. One day, at an Army outpost, he was attacked by a swarm of sand flies. They flew over his bed and injected flesh-eating parasites that cause Leishmaniasis (leesh-muh-NAHY-uh-sis) into his skin. The bites swelled up and oozed like little volcanoes.

A sand fly feeds on human blood. Sand flies also commonly prey on dogs. They live in 88 countries across the world.

A U.S. Army soldier

As the parasites multiplied, the painful bites burst into seeping wounds. Mason sought medical help and soon learned that the treatment could be just as horrible as the disease. Army doctors gave him 20 **injections** of a special drug to fight the parasites. However, the drug made Mason very sick. Eventually, he began to recover from the parasitic infection. Mason was very glad to be rid of the deadly invaders.

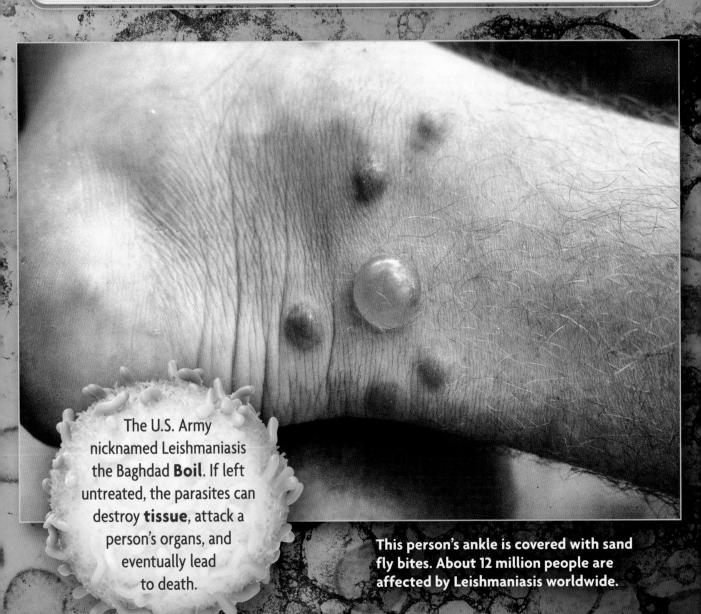

The U.S. Army nicknamed Leishmaniasis the Baghdad **Boil**. If left untreated, the parasites can destroy **tissue**, attack a person's organs, and eventually lead to death.

This person's ankle is covered with sand fly bites. About 12 million people are affected by Leishmaniasis worldwide.

Elephant's Foot Disease

What other diseases are spread by biting flies? One of the most shocking is called elephantiasis (el-uh-fuhn-TAYH-uh-sis), or elephant's foot disease. It's caused by mosquitoes that carry parasitic worms called filaria. When an infected mosquito bites a person, the worms enter the body, multiply, and travel around. They eventually block **vessels** that carry **lymph**, causing fluid to collect in different parts of the body, such as the feet. This can cause limbs to swell to an enormous size.

Filarial worm

A woman suffering from elephantiasis

After an infected mosquito bit Chetan Pithadia, a father in India, his leg began to swell up. Over time, the leg swelled so much that he could barely see his foot. "My condition is getting worse by the day," Chetan said. The leg now weighs over 55 pounds (25 kg), making it hard to walk. While there's no cure for elephantiasis, there's a pill that can prevent it. Chetan wishes he had known about the drug before the filarial worms invaded his body.

A blood-filled mosquito feeding on a person

Elephantiasis mainly affects people in Africa and Asia. More than 120 million people are infected with filarial worms.

Filthy Flies!

Filth flies spread diseases in an entirely different way. Unlike biting flies, they hang around in dirty, smelly places. Common houseflies, for example, eat everything from poop to spoiled food to dead animals. They even feed on human wounds and sores. Some filth flies lay their eggs in the flesh of warm-blooded animals, including humans. The larvae hatch and then eat the flesh!

Houseflies have no teeth and can only eat liquid food. They **vomit** special saliva onto solid food to liquefy it—and then slurp it up.

Houseflies can carry 351 types of bacteria.

As filth flies feed, they pick up and transmit disease-causing **bacteria**. Houseflies, for example, also leave bacteria behind when they poop. Houseflies are so dirty, in fact, that scientists think they carry over 65 different diseases. These diseases range from cholera to leprosy. How can people protect themselves against filth flies? Scientist Jason Tetro recommends two simple things—put uneaten food away, and take the garbage out!

Cleaning up garbage can help control fly numbers.

21

Other Fly-Borne Diseases

In addition to sleeping sickness, river blindness, elephantiasis, and Leishmaniasis, flies can transmit a number of other diseases. Here are some of them:

Anthrax

Anthrax is a serious bacterial disease that affects people and animals. It's often transmitted by stable flies and mosquitoes. Affected people may have blisters or sores on their skin. Anthrax can kill if breathed in or swallowed and not treated quickly.

Anthrax bacteria

Cholera is also spread by drinking water contaminated by cholera bacteria.

Cholera

Cholera is an infection of the intestines. It can be carried by houseflies. The disease causes severe watery diarrhea and vomiting. If not treated, cholera can be deadly.

Leprosy

Leprosy, also known as Hansen's disease (HD), can be transmitted by houseflies. Over time, this disease, which is caused by bacteria, can cause numbness and **paralysis**. Left untreated, leprosy can lead to blindness and disfigurement.

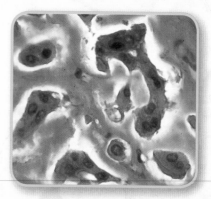

Tissue affected by leprosy bacteria

Glossary

bacteria (bak-TEER-ee-uh) tiny living things that can only be seen with a microscope; some bacteria are helpful while others cause disease

boil (BOIL) an infected lump under the skin

devastating (DEV-uh-stay-ting) shocking or very hard to deal with

encounter (en-KOUN-tur) an unexpected meeting, often unpleasant

eradicating (ih-RAD-uh-kate-ing) eliminating something completely

fatal (FAY-tuhl) deadly

infection (in-FEK-shuhn) an illness caused by germs entering the body

injections (in-JEK-shuns) medical drugs that are administered through a needle

interpreter (in-TUR-prit-uhr) a person who explains what words or information in another language mean

larva (LAR-vuh) a young insect that has a worm-like body

lymph (LIMF) a clear fluid that bathes the cells of the body

maggot (MAG-uht) the worm-like form of a young fly

mammal (MAM-uhl) a warm-blooded animal that usually has fur or hair and feeds its young milk

manure (muh-NYOOR) animal dung

microscope (MYE-kruh-skope) a tool that scientists use to see very small things

paralysis (puh-RAL-uh-siss) the inability to move or feel a part of one's body

parasites (PA-ruh-sites) living things that get food by living on or in another living thing and often cause harm

safari (suh-FAH-ree) a trip taken, especially in Africa, to see large wild animals

sores (SAWRS) very painful places on the body

species (SPEE-sheez) types of animals or plants

tissue (TISH-oo) a group of similar cells that form a part of the body

toxic (TOK-sik) poisonous

vessels (VESS-uhlz) tiny tubes inside the body carrying fluids

vomit (VOM-it) to throw up

wound (WOOND) an injury in which a person's body is cut or damaged

Index

Bibliography

Athas, Eric. "Sand flies infect U.S. forces with parasite that leaves them with 'Baghdad Boil'." *The Washington Post* (June 22, 2010).

Levine, Robert V. "Parasites Are Us." *nautilus.us* (April 21, 2016).

Centers for Disease Control and Prevention: www.cdc.gov

Read More

Owen, Ruth. *Intestines, Zombies, and Jumping Beans: Extraordinary Insect Life Cycles.* New York: Ruby Tuesday (2018).

Seeley, M. H. *Botflies Terrify!* New York: Gareth Stevens (2018).

Learn More Online

To learn more about flies, visit
www.bearportpublishing.com/BuggedOut

About the Author

Alex Giannini is a writer who has always been afraid of spiders. After researching and writing this book, he is now also afraid of botflies.